W9-BXU-889

Some Kids Use Wheelchairs

by Lola M. Schaefer

Consulting Editor: Gail Saunders-Smith, Ph.D.

Consultant: Lawrence Z. Stern, M.D.
Medical Consultant, Muscular Dystrophy Association
Professor of Neurology, University of Arizona

Pebble Books

an imprint of Capstone Press
Mankato, Minnesota

Pebble Books are published by Capstone Press
151 Good Counsel Drive, P.O. Box 669, Mankato, Minnesota 56002
http://www.capstone-press.com

1 2 3 4 5 6 06 05 04 03 02 01

Library of Congress Cataloging-in-Publication Data
Schaefer, Lola M., 1950–
    Some kids use wheelchairs/by Lola M. Schaefer.
    p. cm.—(Understanding differences)
    Includes bibliographical references and index.
    Summary: Simple text and photographs discuss the challenges of using a
wheelchair, why some children cannot walk, and the everyday activities of children
who use wheelchairs.
    ISBN 0-7368-0666-0
    1. Physically handicapped—Transportation—Juvenile literature. 2.
Handicapped—Orientation and mobility—Juvenile literature. 3. Wheelchairs—
Juvenile literature. [1. Physically handicapped. 2. Wheelchairs.] I. Title. II. Series.
    HV3022 .S33 2001
    362.4'3'0973—dc21
                                                                    00-027223

CULTR

Note to Parents and Teachers

The Understanding Differences series supports national social
studies standards related to individual development and identity.
This book describes and illustrates the special needs of children
who use wheelchairs. The photographs support early readers in
understanding the text. The repetition of words and phrases helps
early readers learn new words. This book also introduces early
readers to subject-specific vocabulary words, which are defined in
the Words to Know section. Early readers may need assistance to
read some words and to use the Table of Contents, Words to
Know, Read More, Internet Sites, and Index/Word List sections
of the book.

Table of Contents

Some kids use wheelchairs. Kids who cannot walk use wheelchairs to go places.

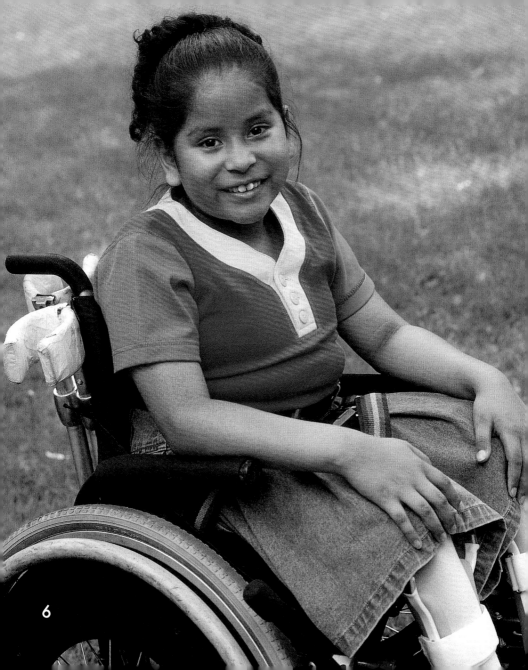

Some kids cannot walk because they were sick or hurt. They may use a wheelchair for a short time or for many years.

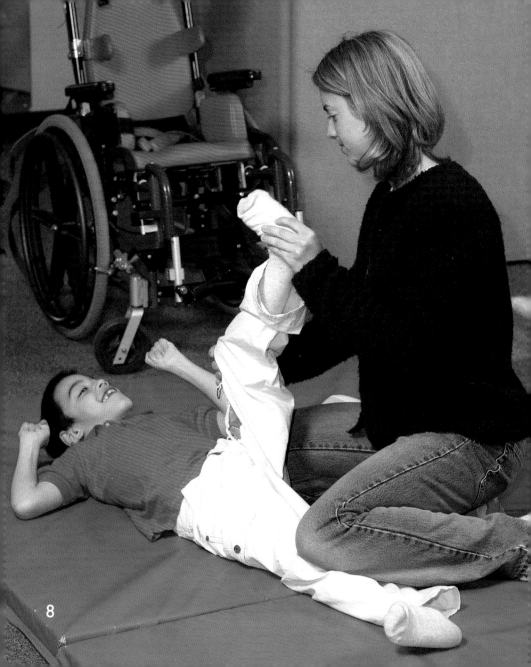

Physical therapists help
kids who use wheelchairs
stretch their muscles.

Some kids who use wheelchairs go swimming. The exercise is good for their muscles.

Some kids who use wheelchairs travel. They use lifts to get into vans.

Some kids who use wheelchairs travel. They use lifts to get into vans.

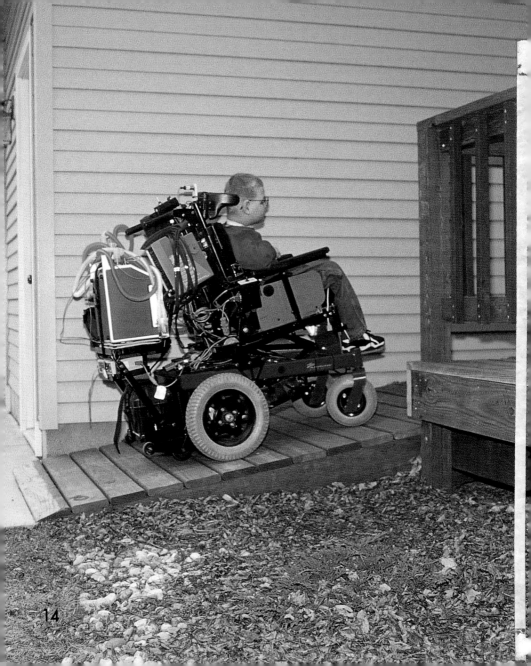

Kids who use wheelchairs go many places. They use ramps to enter buildings.

Some kids who use
wheelchairs go to camp.
They follow trails
through the woods.

Kids who use wheelchairs study. They read books in the library.

Some kids who use wheelchairs play sports. They like to have fun.

Words to Know

lift—a machine used to raise objects; some vans have lifts in them; lifts allow people who use wheelchairs to ride in vans.

physical therapist—a person trained to give treatment to people who are ill, injured, or have physical disabilities; massage and exercise are two kinds of treatment.

ramp—a surface that slants to connect two levels; access ramps provide an entrance into a building or passage between floors of a building.

wheelchair—a type of chair on wheels for people who are ill, injured, or have physical disabilities; wheelchairs can be manual or motorized.

Read More

Bergman, Thomas. *Precious Time: Children Living with Muscular Dystrophy.* Don't Turn Away. Milwaukee: Gareth Stevens, 1996.

Dobkin, Bonnie. *Just a Little Different.* A Rookie Reader. Chicago: Children's Press, 1994.

Keith, Lois. *Being in a Wheelchair.* Think About. Mankato, Minn.: Smart Apple Media, 1999.

Internet Sites

Loving Paws
http://www.lovingpaws.com

Muscular Dystrophy Association
http://www.mdausa.org

Think First
http://www.thinkfirst.org

Index/Word List

buildings, 15
camp, 17
exercise, 11
help, 9
hurt, 7
library, 19
lifts, 13
muscles, 9, 11

physical
  therapists, 9
places, 5, 15
play, 21
ramps, 15
read, 19
sick, 7
sports, 21

stretch, 9
study, 19
swimming, 11
trails, 17
travel, 13
vans, 13
walk, 5, 7
woods, 17

Word Count: 123
Early-Intervention Level: 9

Editorial Credits
Mari C. Schuh, editor; Kia Bielke, designer; Katy Kudela, photo researcher

Photo Credits
Brian and Cindy Braun, 12
David F. Clobes, 14
Eliza Bebler, 1
Gregg R. Andersen, 8
Laura Dwight, cover, 6
Marilyn Moseley LaMantia, 16
Muscular Dystrophy Association, 4, 10, 18, 20

Special thanks to Peter, Cindy, and Brian Braun of Le Sueur, Minnesota, and the children and staff of Pediatric Therapy Services in Mankato, Minnesota, for their assistance with this book.

DATE DUE

MAR 3 1 2002	
MAR 2 7 2003	
MAR 0 4 2004	
MAY 2 4 2004	
SEP 2 0 2006	
MAR 2 0 2009	
MAR 0 1 2023	

GAYLORD   PRINTED IN U.S.A.